Tracing Your Dino

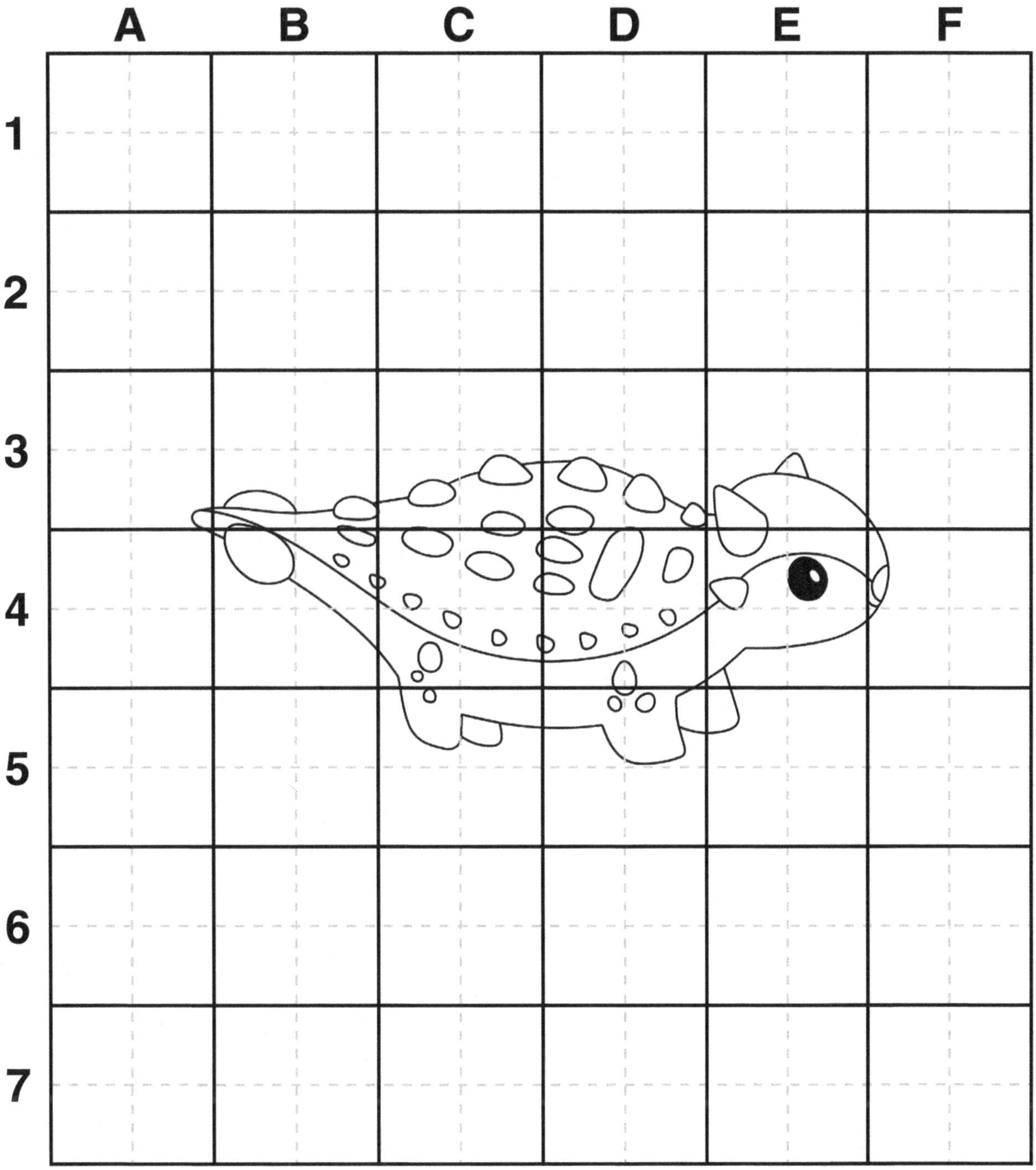

Your draw! Your Dino

<table>
<tr><td></td><td>A</td><td>B</td><td>C</td><td>D</td><td>E</td><td>F</td></tr>
<tr><td>1</td><td></td><td></td><td></td><td></td><td></td><td></td></tr>
<tr><td>2</td><td></td><td></td><td></td><td></td><td></td><td></td></tr>
<tr><td>3</td><td></td><td></td><td></td><td></td><td></td><td></td></tr>
<tr><td>4</td><td></td><td></td><td></td><td></td><td></td><td></td></tr>
<tr><td>5</td><td></td><td></td><td></td><td></td><td></td><td></td></tr>
<tr><td>6</td><td></td><td></td><td></td><td></td><td></td><td></td></tr>
<tr><td>7</td><td></td><td></td><td></td><td></td><td></td><td></td></tr>
</table>

Coloring Your Dino

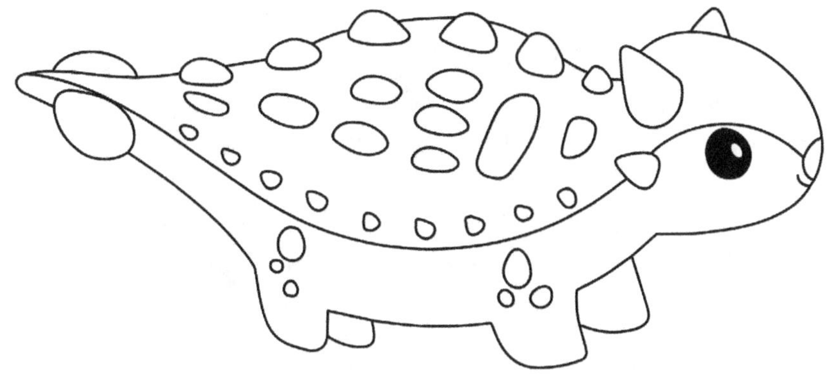

Make perfect! Your Dino

Tracing Your Dino

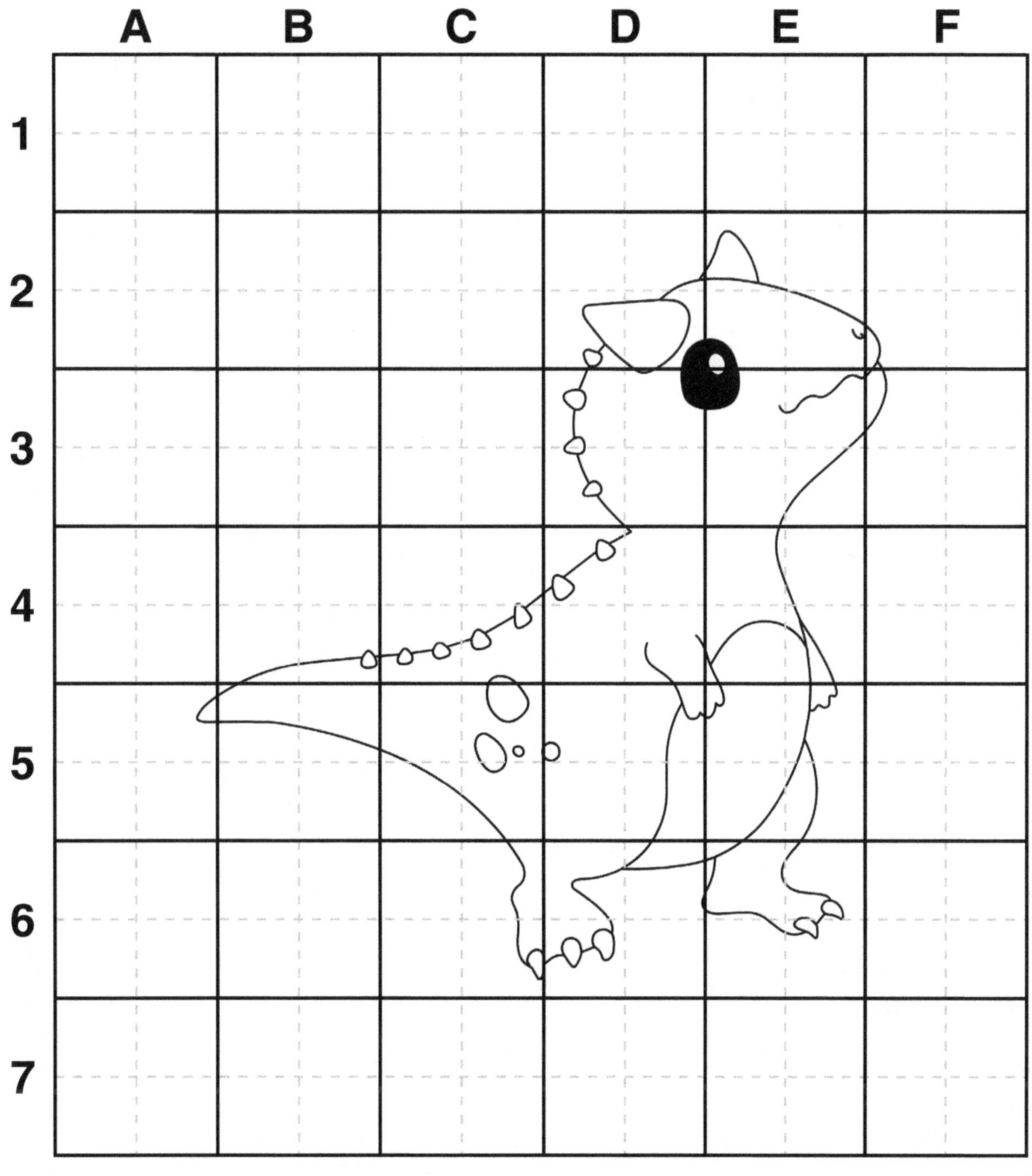

Your draw! Your Dino

	A	B	C	D	E	F
1						
2						
3						
4						
5						
6						
7						

Coloring Your Dino

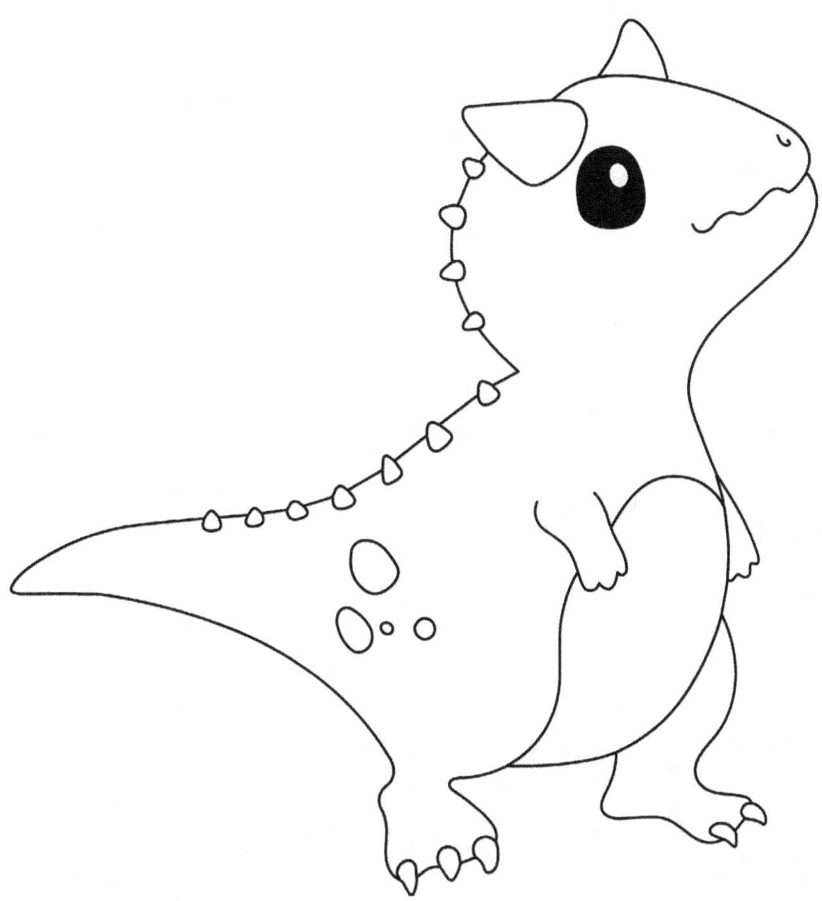

Make perfect! Your Dino

Tracing Your Dino

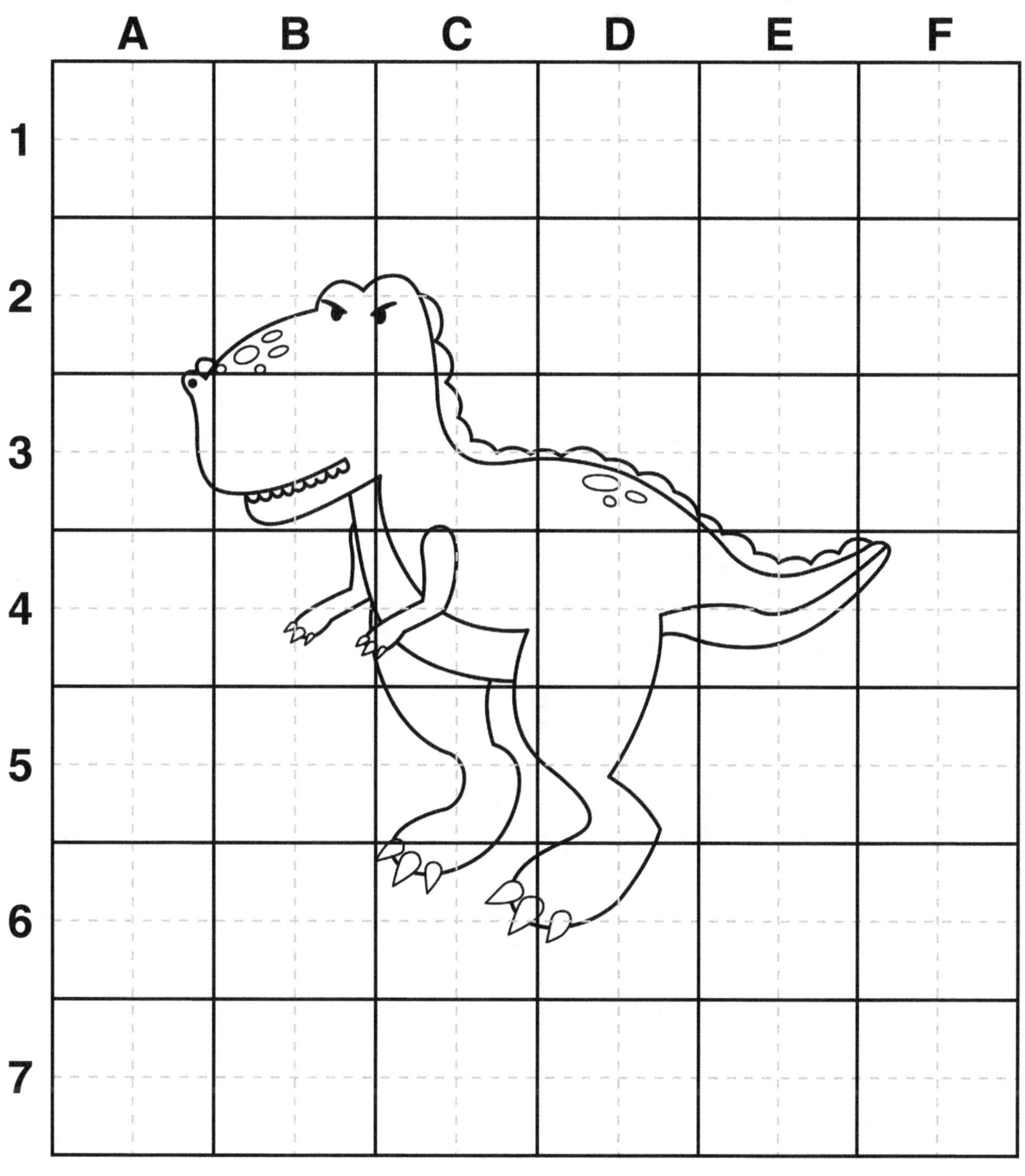

Your draw! Your Dino

	A	B	C	D	E	F
1						
2						
3						
4						
5						
6						
7						

Coloring Your Dino

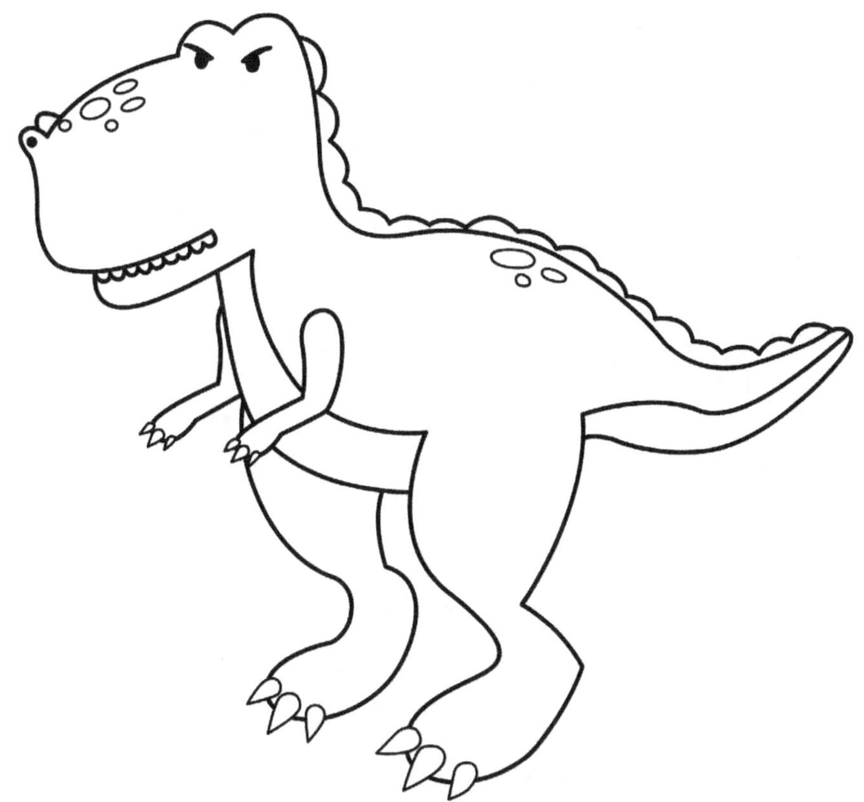

Make perfect! Your Dino

Tracing Your Dino

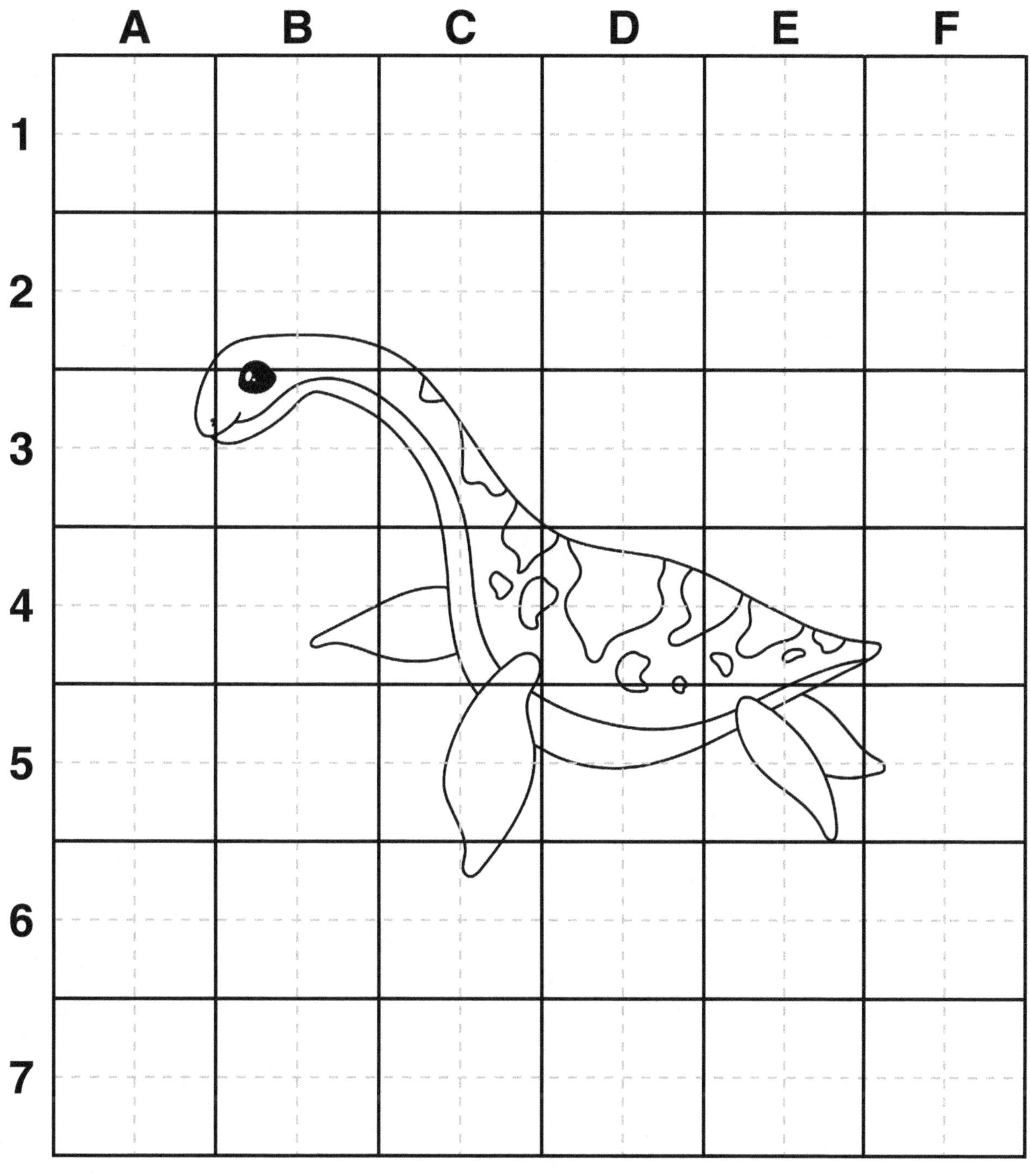

Your draw! Your Dino

	A	B	C	D	E	F
1						
2						
3						
4						
5						
6						
7						

Coloring Your Dino

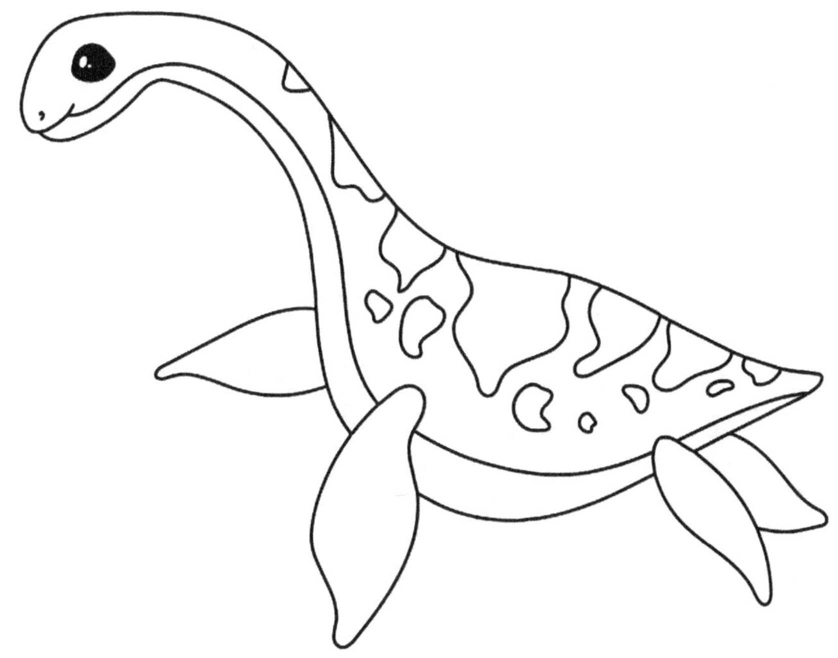

Make perfect! Your Dino

Tracing Your Dino

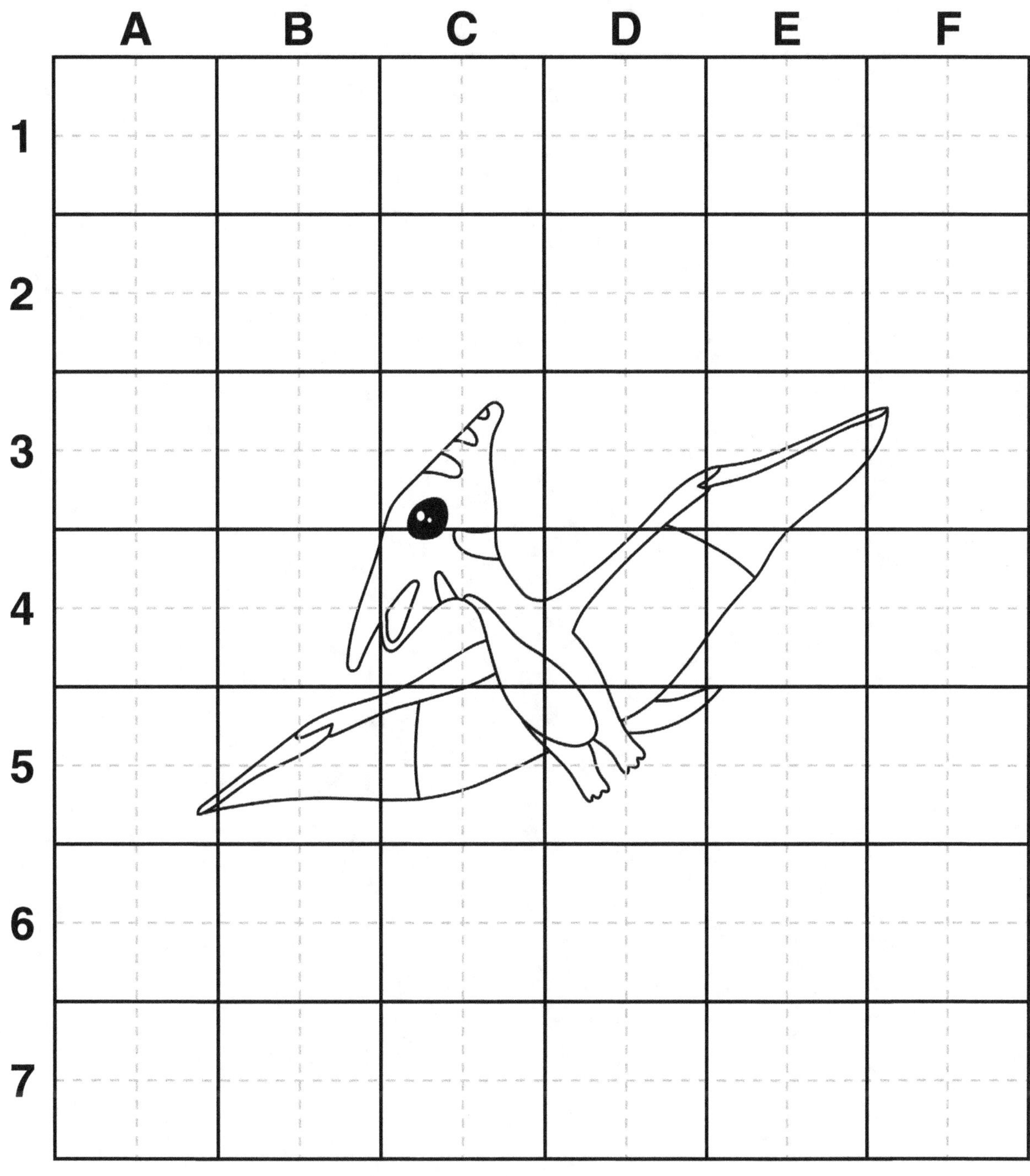

Your draw! Your Dino

	A	B	C	D	E	F
1						
2						
3						
4						
5						
6						
7						

Coloring Your Dino

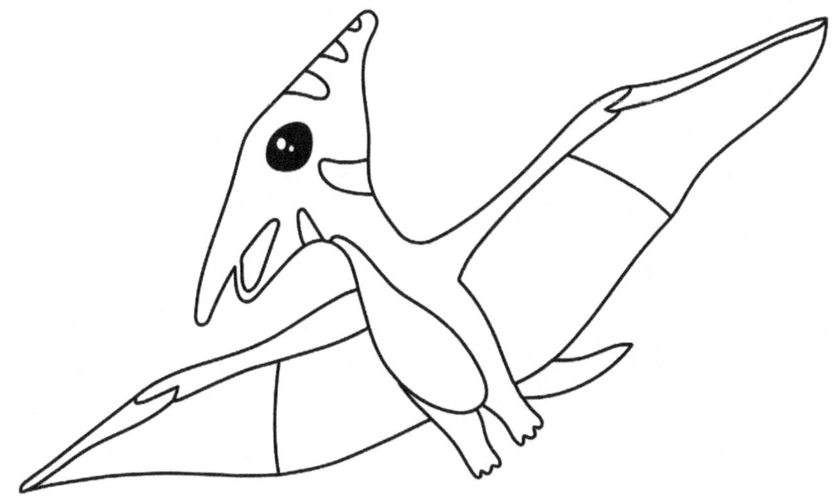

Make perfect! Your Dino

Tracing Your Dino

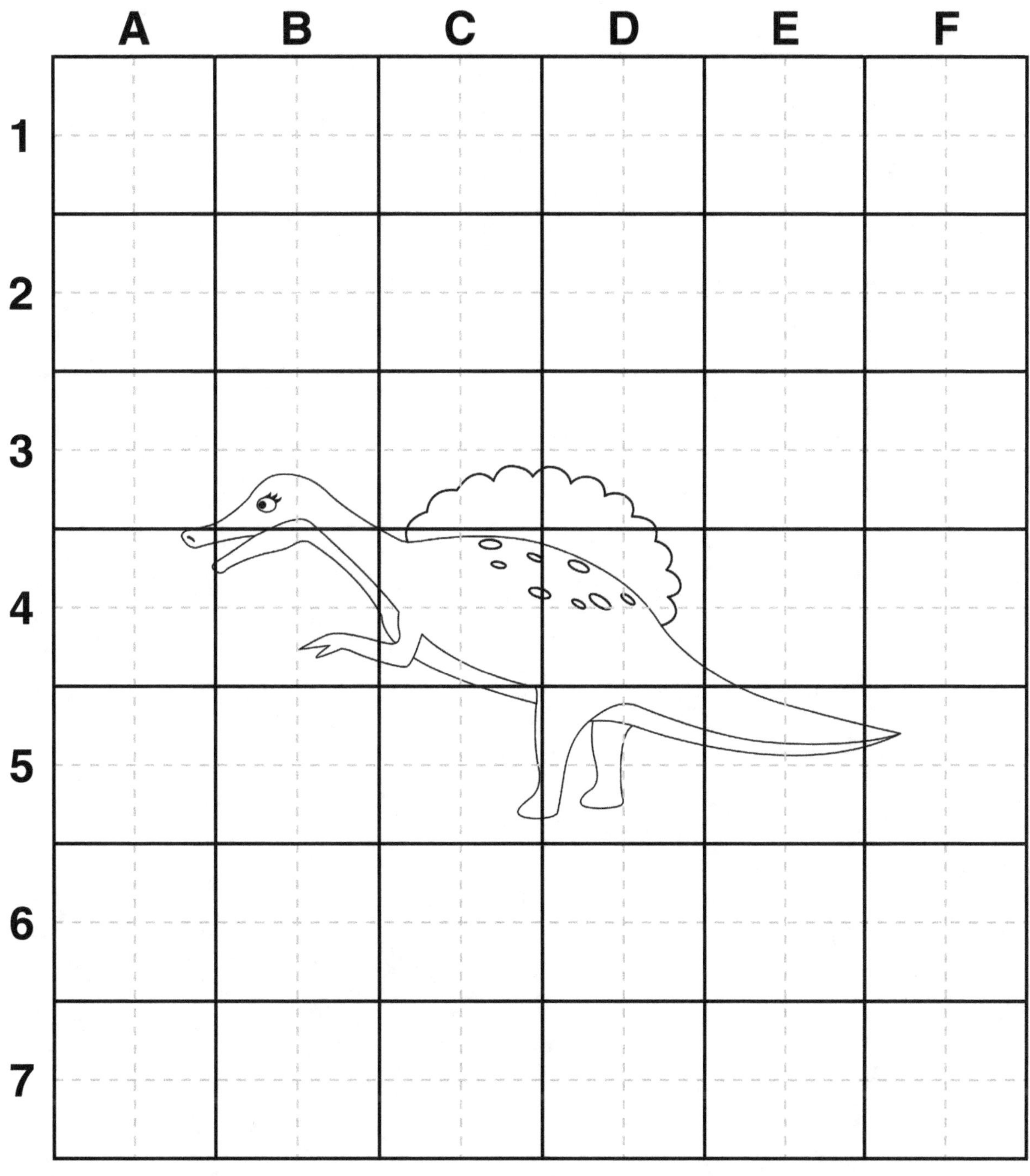

Your draw! Your Dino

	A	B	C	D	E	F
1						
2						
3						
4						
5						
6						
7						

Coloring Your Dino

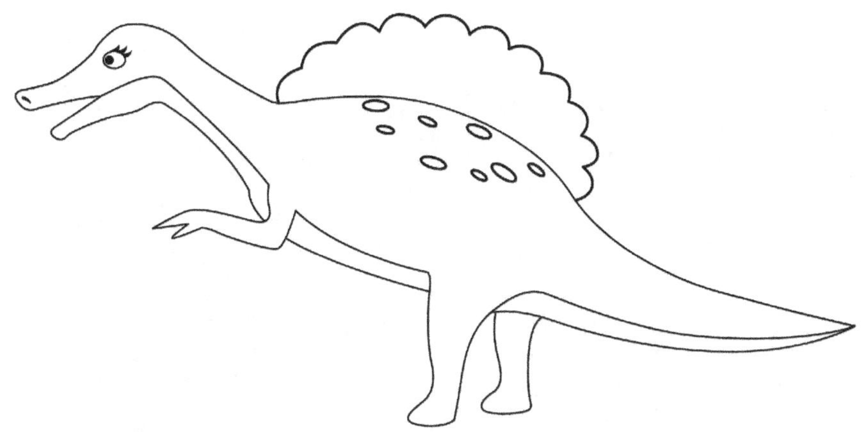

Make perfect! Your Dino

Tracing Your Dino

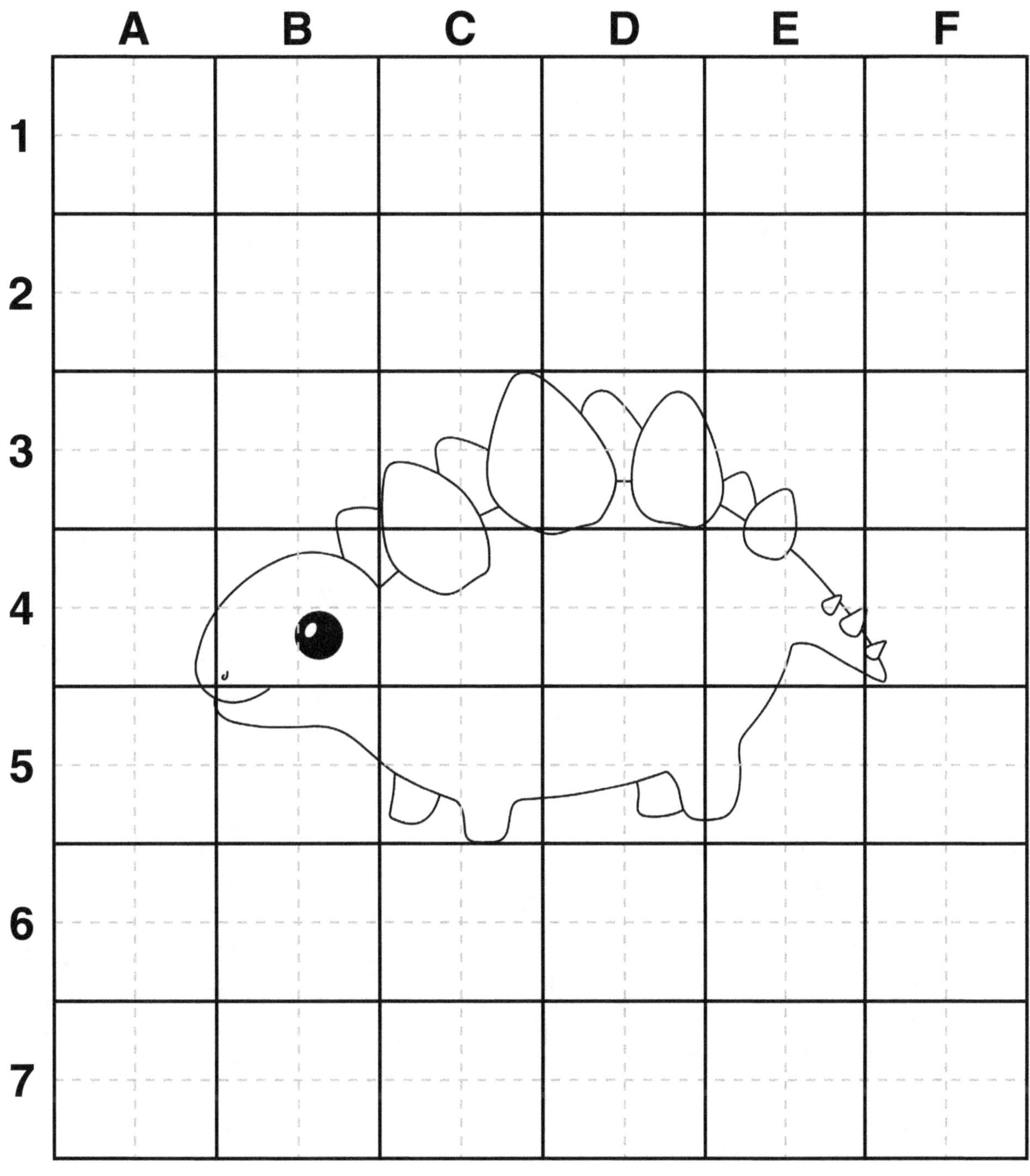

Your draw! Your Dino

	A	B	C	D	E	F
1						
2						
3						
4						
5						
6						
7						

Coloring Your Dino

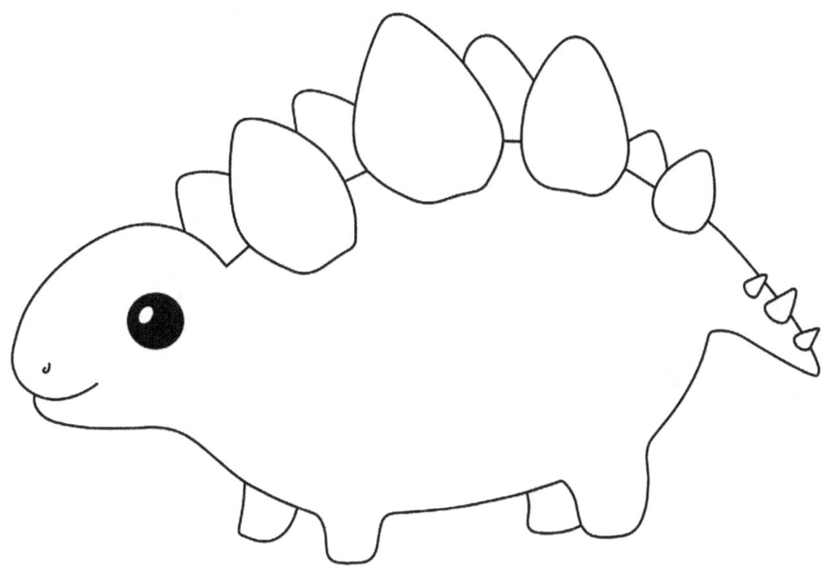

Make perfect! Your Dino

Tracing Your Dino

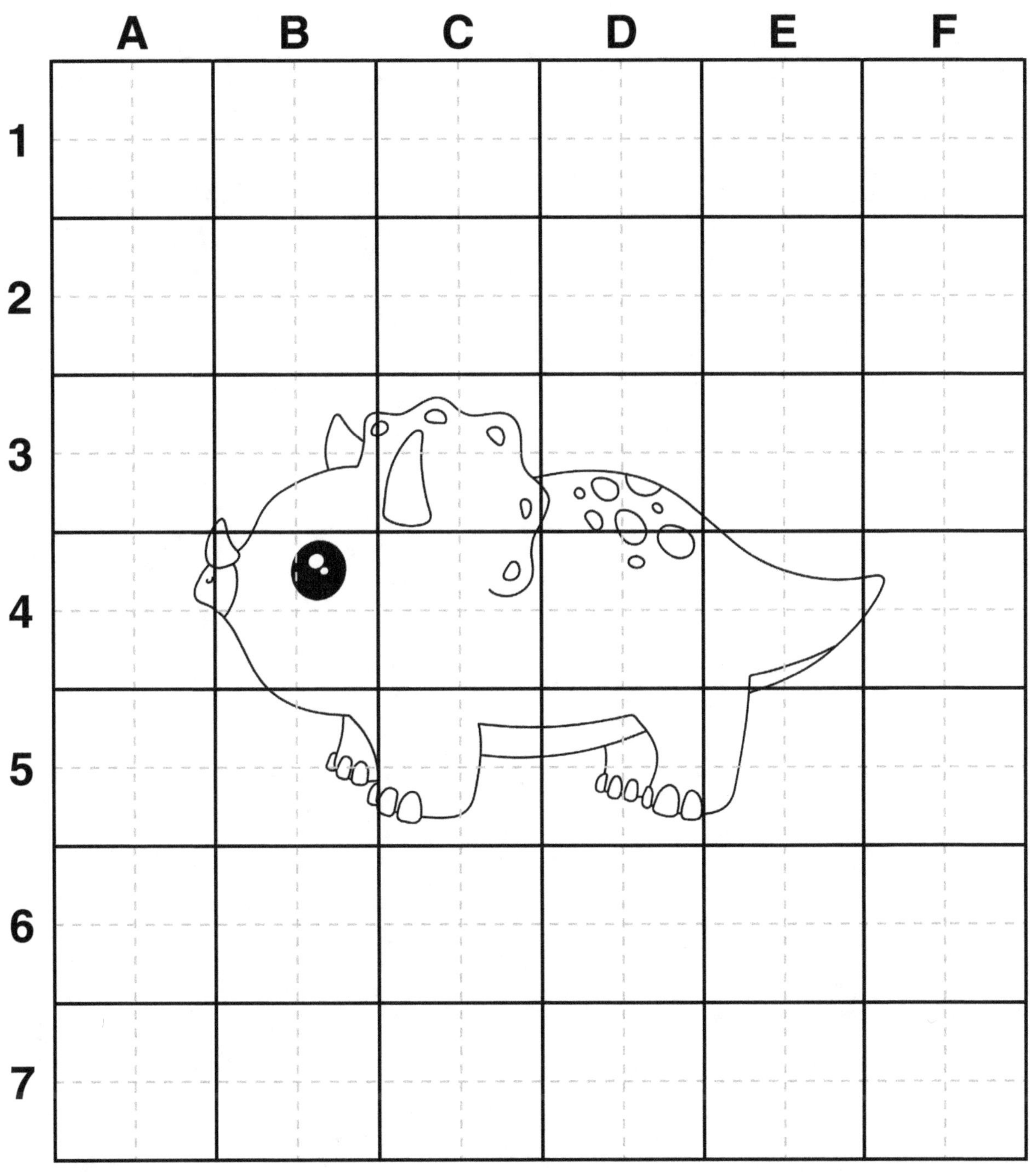

Your draw! Your Dino

	A	B	C	D	E	F
1						
2						
3						
4						
5						
6						
7						

Coloring Your Dino

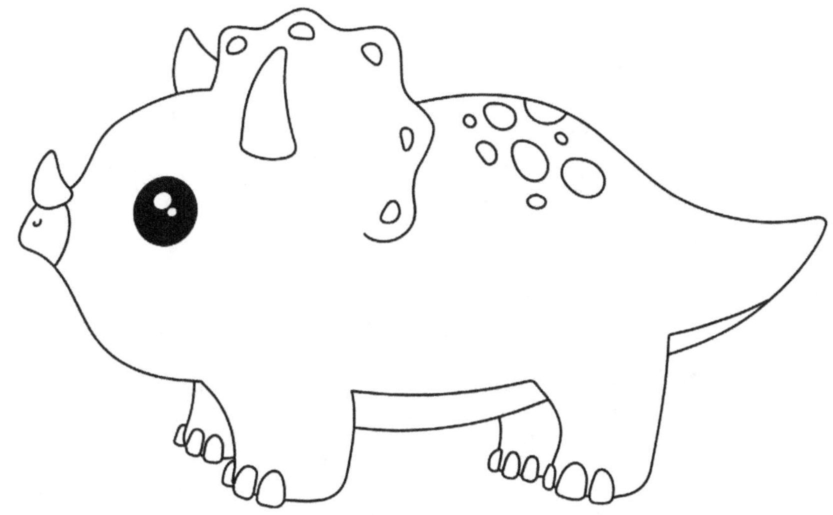

Make perfect! Your Dino

Tracing Your Dino

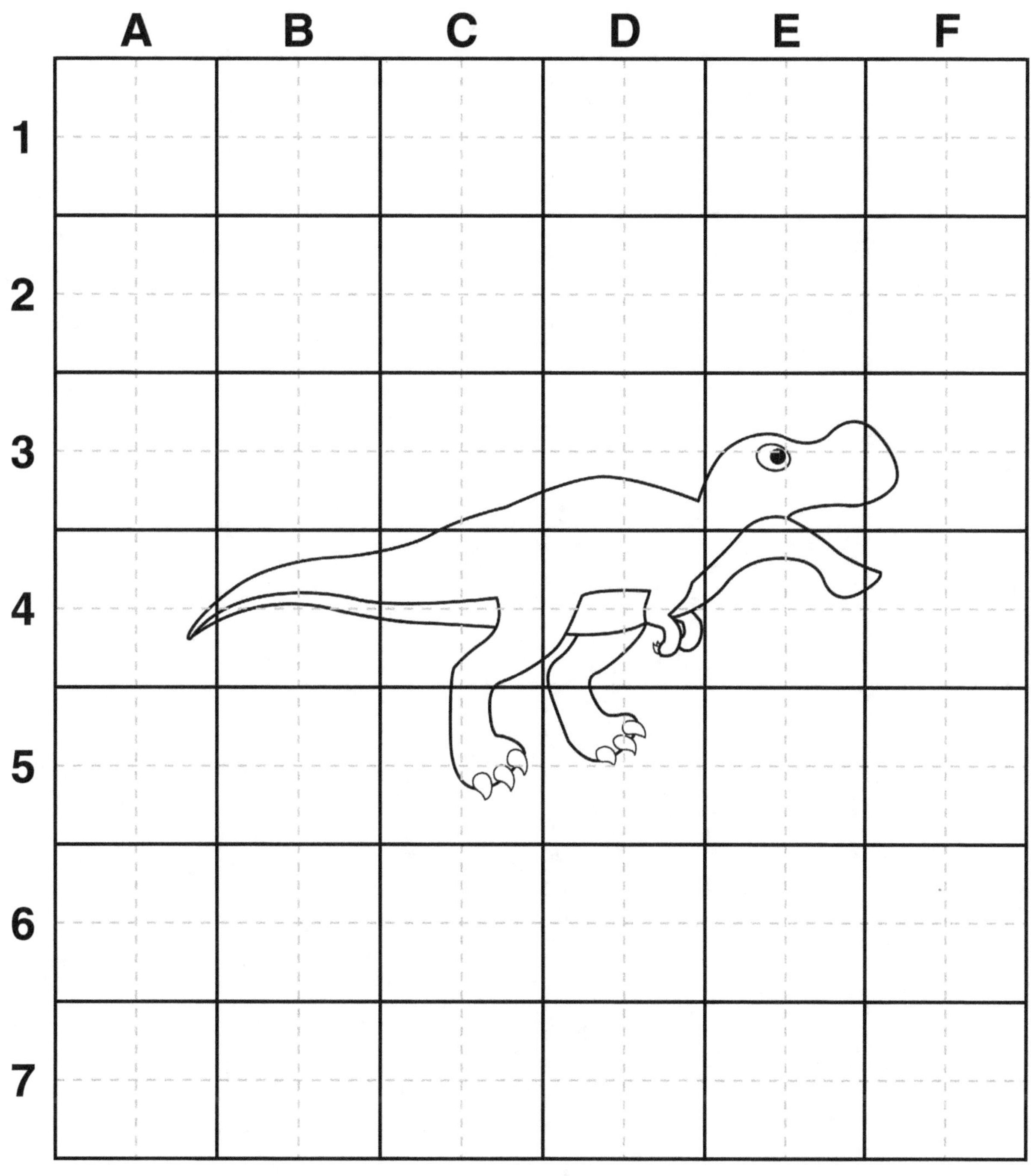

Your draw! Your Dino

	A	B	C	D	E	F
1						
2						
3						
4						
5						
6						
7						

Coloring Your Dino

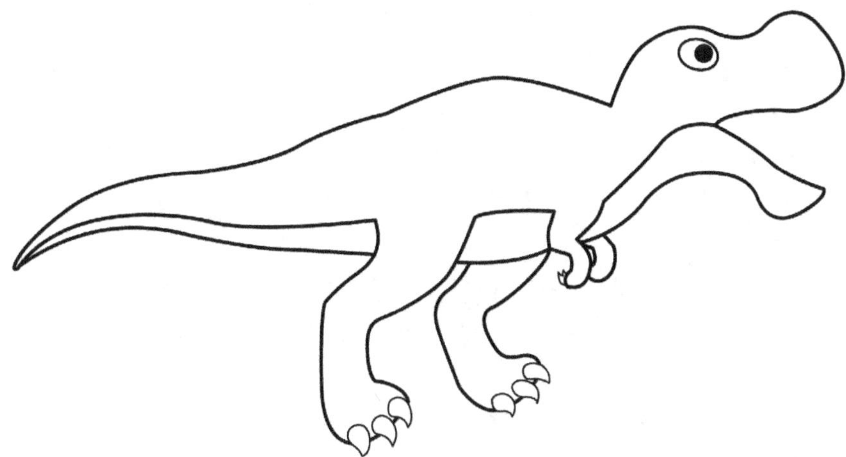

Make perfect! Your Dino

Tracing Your Dino

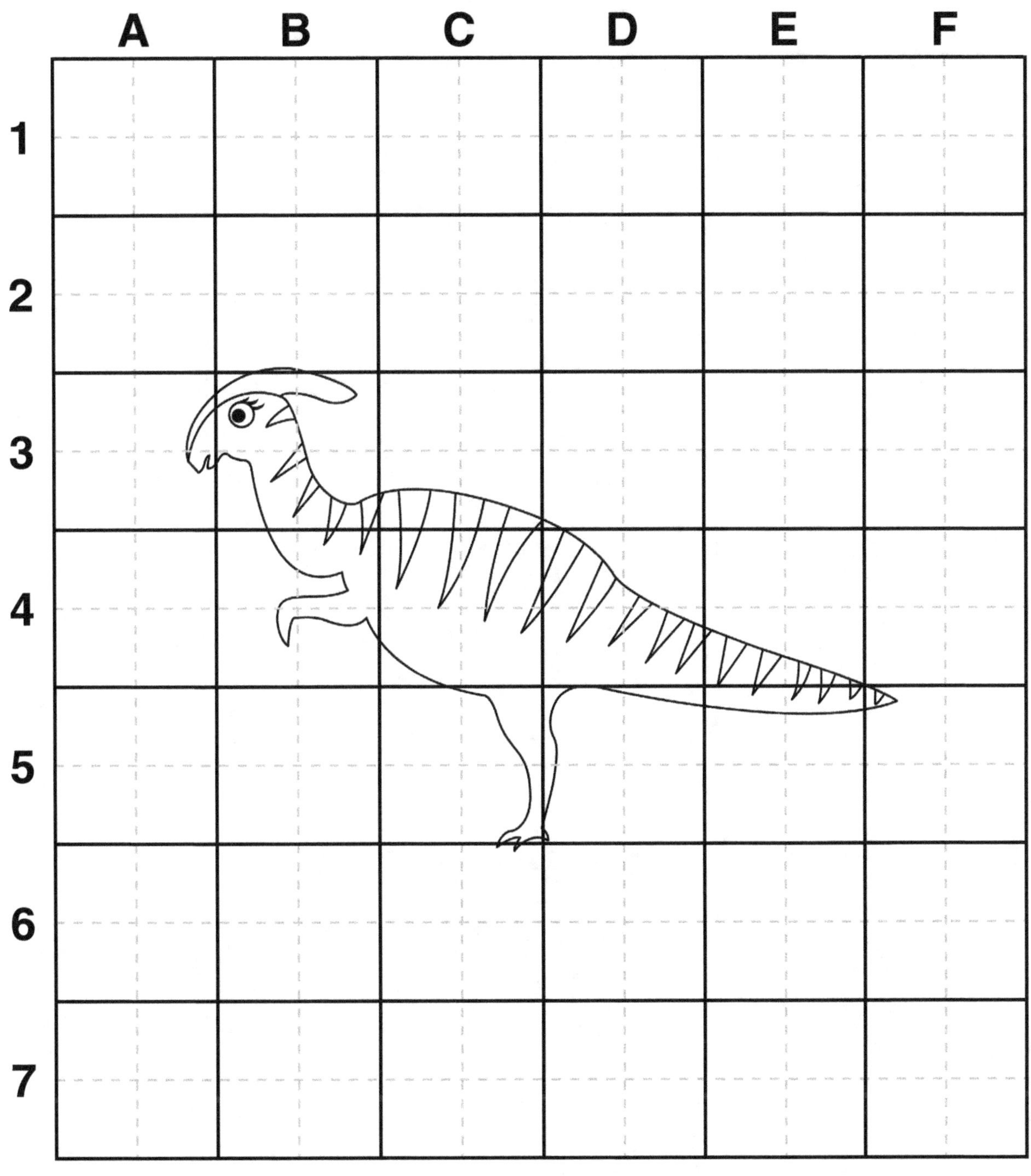

Your draw! Your Dino

<table>
<tr><th></th><th>A</th><th>B</th><th>C</th><th>D</th><th>E</th><th>F</th></tr>
<tr><td>1</td><td></td><td></td><td></td><td></td><td></td><td></td></tr>
<tr><td>2</td><td></td><td></td><td></td><td></td><td></td><td></td></tr>
<tr><td>3</td><td></td><td></td><td></td><td></td><td></td><td></td></tr>
<tr><td>4</td><td></td><td></td><td></td><td></td><td></td><td></td></tr>
<tr><td>5</td><td></td><td></td><td></td><td></td><td></td><td></td></tr>
<tr><td>6</td><td></td><td></td><td></td><td></td><td></td><td></td></tr>
<tr><td>7</td><td></td><td></td><td></td><td></td><td></td><td></td></tr>
</table>

Coloring Your Dino

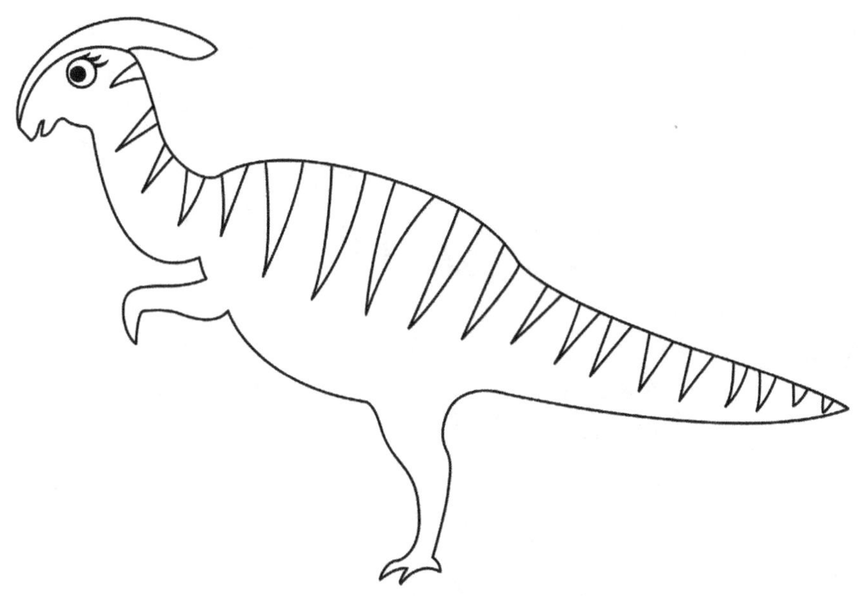

Make perfect! Your Dino

Tracing Your Dino

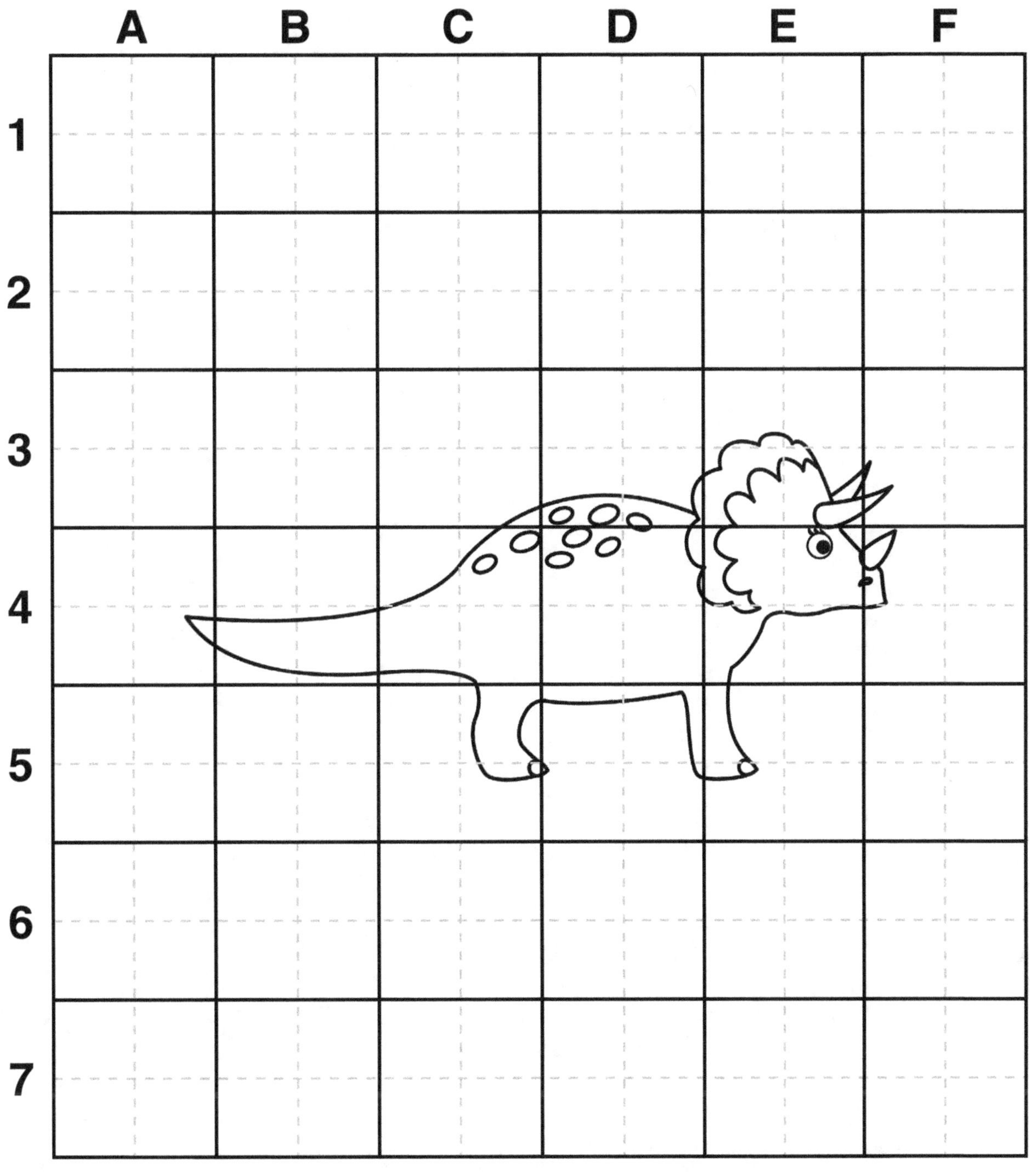

Your draw! Your Dino

Coloring Your Dino

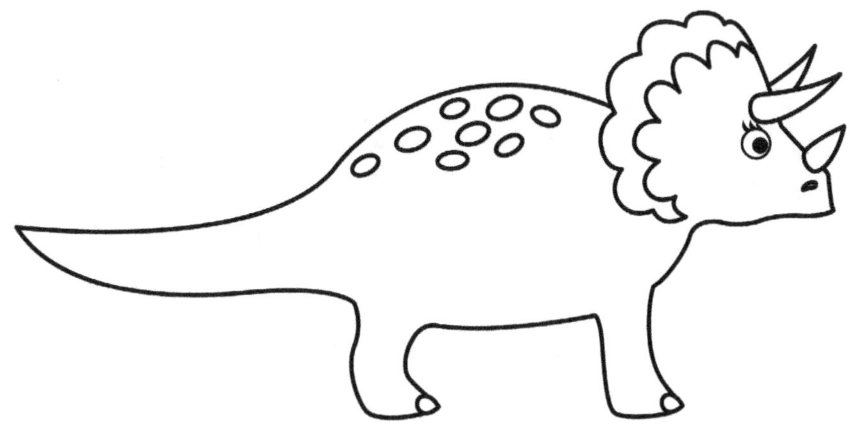

Make perfect! Your Dino

Tracing Your Dino

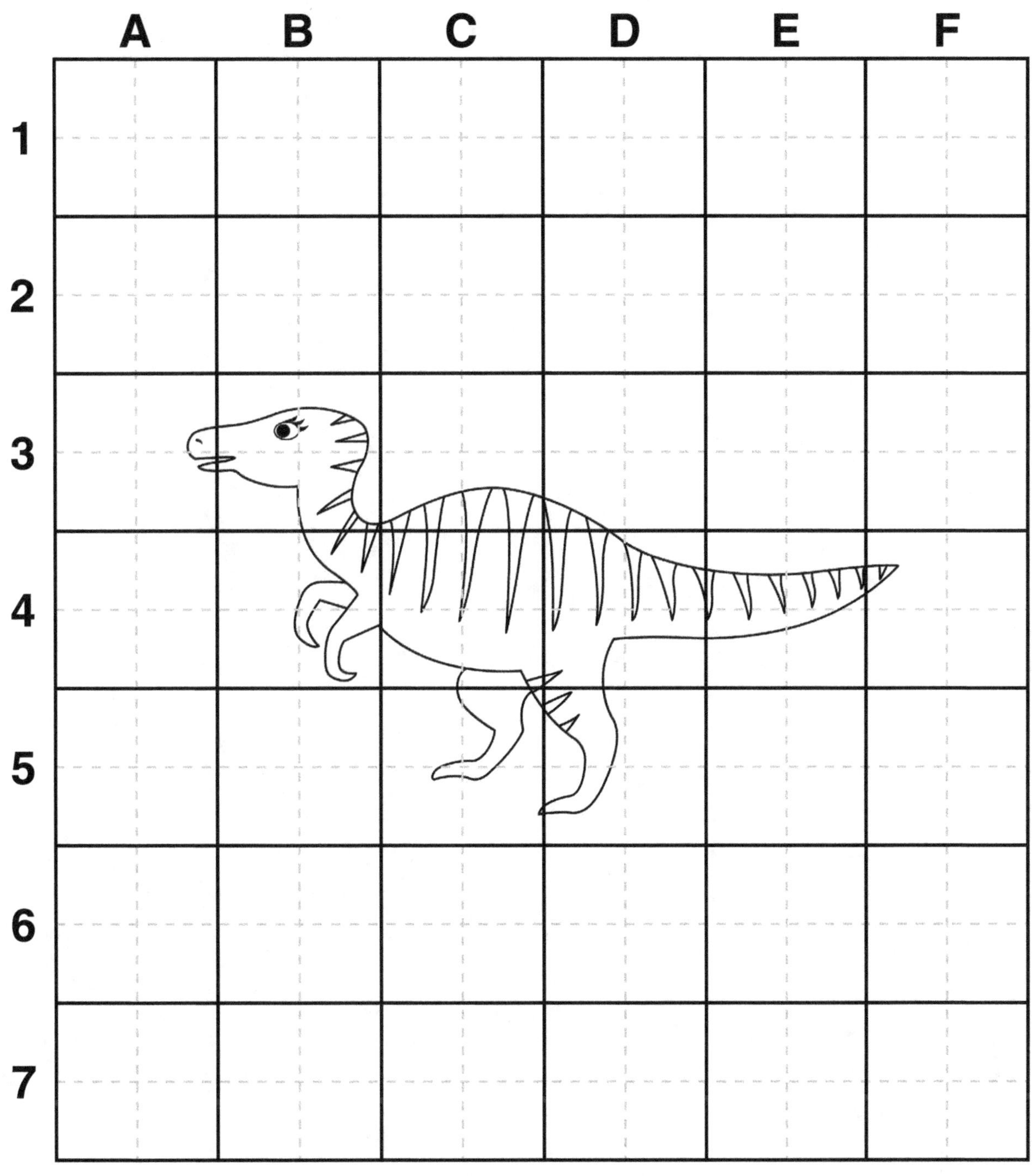

Your draw! Your Dino

Coloring Your Dino

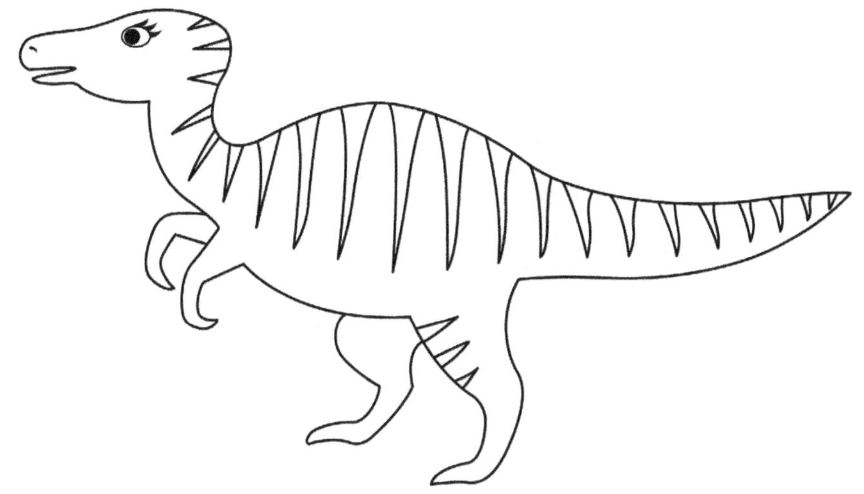

Make perfect! Your Dino